A Frog Has a Sticky Tongue

Pamela Graham

A **frog** has a sticky tongue

and a **frog** has big eyes.

What else has big eyes?

A **tiger** has big eyes

and a **tiger** has whiskers.

What else has whiskers?

An **otter** has whiskers

and an **otter** has webbed feet.

What else has webbed feet?

A **penguin** has webbed feet

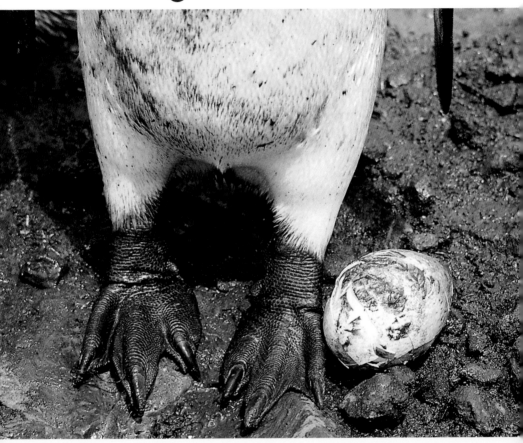

and a **penguin** has a beak.

What else has a beak?

An **ostrich** has a beak

and an **oStrich** has a long neck.

What else has a long neck?

A **giraffe** has a long neck

and a **giraffe** has horns.

What else has horns?

A **goat** has horns

and a **goat** has a hairy body.

What else has a hairy body?

A **moth** has a hairy body

and a **moth** has wings.

What else has wings?

A **bee** has wings

and a **bee** has stripes.

What else has stripes?

A **lionfish** has stripes

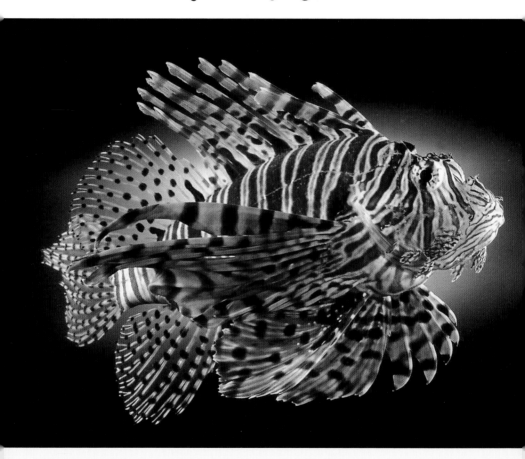

and a **lionfish** has spines.

What else has spines?

An **echidna** has spines

and an **echidna** has
a sticky tongue.

What else has a sticky tongue?

A **frog** has a sticky tongue.